A Ladybird Book
Series 606A

This is the third book in the Ladybird 'Easy-Reading' series. Like the other titles in this series, this book has been specially planned and written to encourage that extra reading practice so necessary before a child can read with ease.

The text is set in large clear type, the vocabulary has been carefully chosen by an expert, and the story of the Nativity has been very beautifully illustrated.

The Baby Jesus

retold for easy reading
by HILDA I. ROSTRON

illustrated by CLIVE UPTTON

Ladybird Books Loughborough

BABY JESUS

Mary was kind and good. She lived in a small, white house in Nazareth. The house had a flat roof. There were stone steps at the side of the house. Mary could climb the steps on to the roof.

If Mary looked down from the roof, she would see the children playing. Mary loved children.

4

One day Mary was busy in her home. She sang as she worked. Then Mary sat down to rest.

As she sat still, the room became very bright. Mary looked up and saw an angel. The angel said:

"God is sending a Baby Son to you. You shall call His name Jesus."

When the angel had gone, Mary was very happy. She was so glad God was sending her Baby Jesus.

Mary had a cousin in the hill country of Juda. Her name was Elizabeth.

"I must go and see Elizabeth and let her know about my Baby," thought Mary.

So Mary went to see Elizabeth.

One day Joseph told Mary that they had to go to Bethlehem. Many other people were going, too.

So Mary packed clothes and food. She rode on a donkey, and Joseph walked by the side.

The little donkey's feet went clip-clop-clip-clop along the road. Up and down hills and round twisty bends.

After a long time, Mary was tired. The donkey was tired, too. Joseph was tired. They would be glad when they got to Bethlehem.

At last they were there.

Mary knew her Baby would be born soon. She hoped they could find a place to rest.

Joseph knocked at a door.

"Have you any room for us to stay?" he asked. The man who opened the door shook his head.

"Sorry, no room here," he said.

No one had a room to spare.

Many people were staying in Bethlehem.

Joseph knocked at the door of an inn.

"Have you any room for us?" asked Joseph. The inn-keeper saw tired Mary on the donkey.

"I've no room here; but you can stay in the stable," he said.

Joseph thanked him, and they went into the stable.

The stable was clean and warm and quiet. Oxen were there, and they stared at the little donkey eating his supper.

Joseph made a soft bed of hay for Mary to lie on. He unpacked the food and clothes.

That night Mary's Baby was born in the stable. She called His name, Jesus.

Mother Mary wrapped Baby Jesus in a shawl. Then she laid Him in the manger.

The manger was the place where the hay was put for the animals. It was soft and warm for the Baby.

Mary smiled and was so happy. She said "Thank You" to God for sending Baby Jesus.

There were green hills near Bethlehem. On the hills shepherds looked after their sheep. When it was dark they lit a big fire to keep themselves warm.

The fire kept away wild animals from harming the sheep and lambs.

The shepherds watched their sheep all day and all night.

One night when they were watching, a big, bright light shone in the sky.

The shepherds were afraid at first. Then they heard angels singing. One angel told the shepherds not to be afraid:

"I have good news for you. Jesus is born in Bethlehem. You will find Him lying in a manger," said the angel.

After the singing angels had gone, the shepherds talked about the good news.

"Let us go to Bethlehem," they said, "and see what has happened."

They hurried down the hill as fast as they could.

One shepherd stayed behind to mind the sheep and lambs.

The shepherds came to Bethlehem and ran down the street to the Inn. There was a light in the stable.

"This must be the place," said the first shepherd. He tapped at the door and peeped in.

It *was* the place. The shepherds found Mary and Joseph. The Baby Jesus was lying in the manger.

Mary and Joseph smiled at the shepherds. They tip-toed near to see the Baby Jesus.

The shepherds told of the light and the angels. They told of the singing, and of hearing the good news.

Mary listened.

The shepherds thanked God for sending Baby Jesus. Then they said "Good-bye" and tip-toed away.

As soon as the shepherds were out of the stable, they talked about what they had seen.

They told everyone about Mary and Joseph, and about the Baby Jesus in the stable. The people told others the good news.

They were all glad. The shepherds sang for joy as they went back to their sheep.

Some time later, while Jesus was still only a baby, there lived three Wise Men in a far off Eastern land. They watched the stars and talked about them.

The Wise Men were looking for a new star.

"When God makes a new star to shine, it will mean that there is a new Baby King," said the Wise Men.

One night the three Wise Men were watching the stars. There were many stars to see.

Then one Wise Man said:

"Look, there is a new star!"

The other two Wise Men looked up.

"Yes," they said, "it *is* a new star. It is so bright. It must be the star of the Baby King!"

"Let us follow the new star and find the Baby King," said one of the three Wise Men.

"Yes," said the others, "and we will take three presents with us."

So they packed the best gifts they could find. When all was ready they climbed on their camels and rode away.

On, and on, and on went the camels. They came to a place where there was nothing but sand. It was hard to find the right way to go.

The Wise Men stopped to rest.

"We will wait for the bright star to shine," they said. That night they saw it.

They were *so* glad. They followed where it led.

At last the Wise Men came to a palace in Jerusalem.

"He must be here," said the Wise Men. They asked King Herod in the palace where the Baby King was. But he did not know.

The king asked his clever men, who said:

"Our books say the Baby King was born in Bethlehem."

Joseph and Mary and Baby Jesus now lived in a little house in Bethlehem.

The Wise Men had to find where He lived. And there the bright star was shining when the Wise Men came to Bethlehem. It was shining right over the little house.

So the Wise Men stopped their camels.

They got off their camels. Then they took their three presents into the little house.

There was Jesus on His mother's knee. Jesus was the Baby King. The Wise Men had followed His star.

They knelt down and gave to Him their gifts of gold, frankincense and myrrh.

His mother thanked them, and the Baby King smiled.

The Wise Men said "Good-bye" to Baby Jesus and Mary and Joseph.

They got on to their camels and rode home. They were so glad God had sent a star to show the way to the Baby King.

The camels went on, and on, and on, back to the homes of the Three Wise Men.

A CHRISTMAS CAROL

Away in a manger, no crib
    for a bed,

The little Lord Jesus laid down
    His sweet head.

The stars in the bright sky
    looked down where He lay—

The little Lord Jesus asleep
    on the hay.